Water Colors

THE PHOTOGRAPHS OF MICHAEL S. MAURER

Water Colors

THE PHOTOGRAPHS OF MICHAEL S. MAURER

for Janie

Published and distributed by IBJ Corp. Contract Publishing
41 E. Washington St., Suite 200; Indianapolis, IN 46204
317-634-6200; 317-263-5402 (fax)

Printed by Graphic Arts Center Indianapolis,
a division of Mail-Well

IBJ CORP. CONTRACT PUBLISHING

Library of Congress Card Catalog

ISBN 0-9745673-0-2

Printed and bound in the United States of America

First Edition

Inquiries regarding the photographs may be directed to Michael S. Maurer at mmaurer@ibj.com.

JACKET FRONT: Hinge-beak Shrimp in Soft Coral
JACKET BACK: File Clam
PREVIOUS PAGE: Anemone Shrimp

Bicolor Blenny

Water Colors

THE PHOTOGRAPHS OF MICHAEL S. MAURER

Many of the subjects in this book are no larger than the eye of the great white.

Great White Shark. Photo taken from inside a cage off the coast of South Africa.
Thank you Chad Henning, friend and fellow diver, for the assist on this shot.

We approach the reef with
respect for the home of some of
God's most beautiful creatures.
We are guests in this home.
We will photograph the smallest
of the animals living here
and leave them in peace.

–MSM

*"I drifted downward
and easily
along the light current,
completely lost
to the world above."*

ABOVE AND RIGHT:

Solomon Islands reef photographed by friend and fellow diver
Ingo Rieck of Dortmund, Germany

A Dangerous Experiment

$\mathcal{W}$e were relaxing on the beach the last day of our Acapulco vacation when a young boy approached the shore in a small motorboat. Would we be interested in water sports? Fishing? Para-sailing? Scuba diving?

This was the early '70s. We knew nothing about scuba diving.

Our flight was to depart late that afternoon. We had some time so my wife, Janie, and I and our friend Doug Popp elected scuba diving.

Royal Gramma

Clownfish in Anemone

In the middle of the bay, the boy helped us don fins, masks, weight belts and tanks – no instructions, no safety equipment. Just jump in and breathe. That's exactly what Doug did, leaving Janie and me on the boat laughing at each other and wondering what to do. We slipped over the side and held onto the boat. Cautiously, I lowered my face into the water and was awed by the panorama of activity. Without a further thought, I let go of the boat and drifted downward and easily along the light current, completely lost to the world above. I was enthralled.

Peppermint Goby

Porcelain Crab beneath Anemone

I relaxed, kicking leisurely, not realizing the distance from my entry point was increasing as my air supply was ebbing. Suddenly, the air that was so freely flowing became much tougher to access. I correctly assumed my adventure was coming to a forced end, so I surfaced, expecting to reach out for the safety of the small motorboat. Much to my surprise, the boat was a speck on the horizon. The sight was a jolting return to reality.

Fortunately, I was spotted and rescued just as I was about to ditch the weight belt and other paraphernalia that had led to such transfixed joy. As soon as I returned to landlocked Indiana, I enrolled in a scuba-diving class and became a certified diver. It was through these lessons that I learned how many different ways I could have killed myself on that first dive.

By the way, Janie never did relinquish her grip on the boat. She always has been the smarter half.

Juvenile Striped Catfish

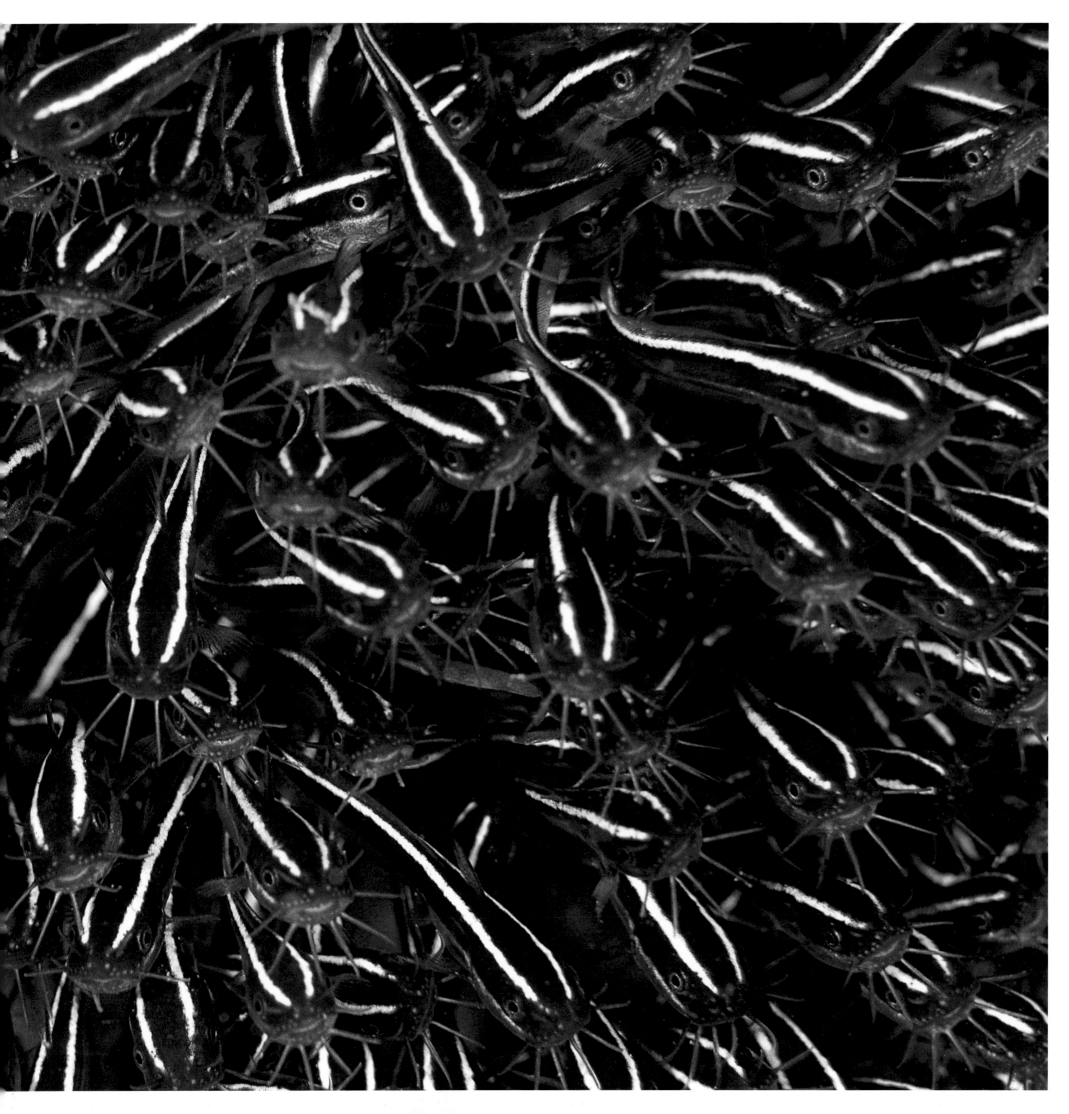

Look closely.

Cave Coral Shrimp

Blue-tipped Starfish on Soft Coral

Tiger Sea Whip Goby on Sea Whip Coral

Coleman Shrimp on Fire Urchin

Turquoise Scorpion Fish

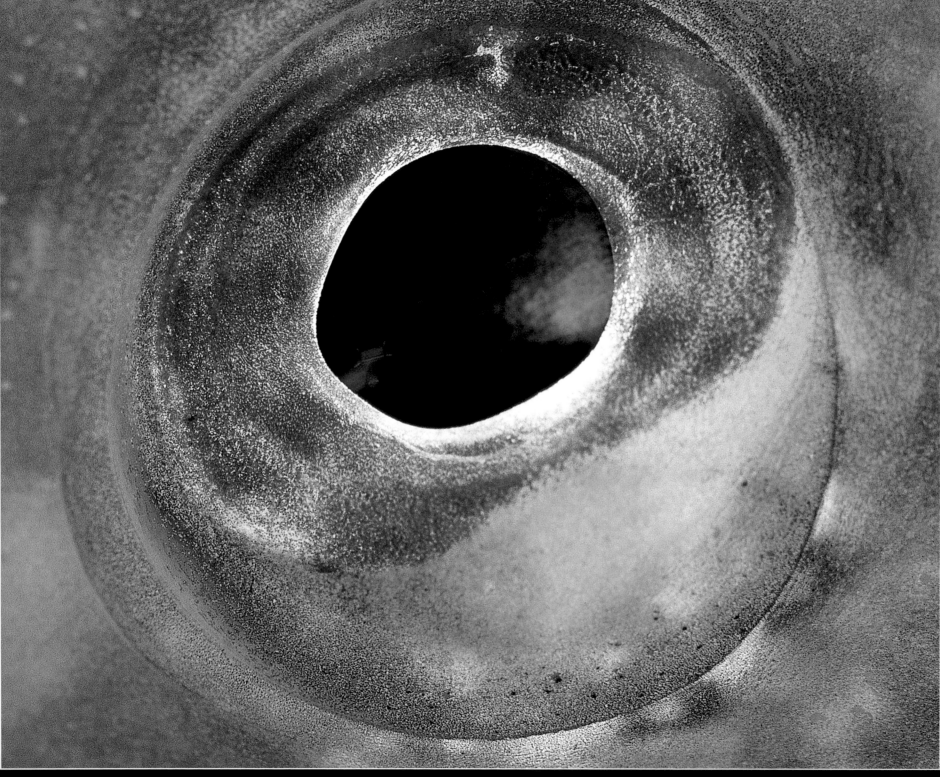

Parrot Fish detail

Orange Spotted Goby

Merlet Scorpion Fish

Developing an Eye

Clownfish in Anemone (left and above)

Once in the early '80s, I rented an underwater camera. I have rarely dived without one in hand since.

The early pictures were fun to show to friends curious about the underwater world, but they were hardly works of art. (I threw them away long ago.)

On the advice of Bob Mayes, the dean of scuba-diving instructors in Indianapolis, I traveled with my friend Harvey Berkey to Islamorada, Florida, to take lessons from photo pro Chris McLaughlin. We concentrated on maximizing the potential of the Nikonos V. This Nikon product is a self-contained, underwater camera with an accompanying set of strobes, tubes and framers that billed itself as virtually idiot-proof. I wanted to test that theory. Under McLaughlin's tutelage, Harvey and I learned to take credible pictures, a few of which appear in this volume.

I used to recommend this gear to beginners. It is light, with no separate housing to worry about. It is, in fact, idiot-proof. But Nikon has discontinued the Nikonos line.

This is unfortunate. Although the Nikonos V is not as sophisticated or flexible as a housed single-lens-reflex camera, it is capable of very fine work and is compatible with several lenses. In fact, the Nikonos V with a 15-millimeter lens remains the choice of many pros for wide-angle photography.

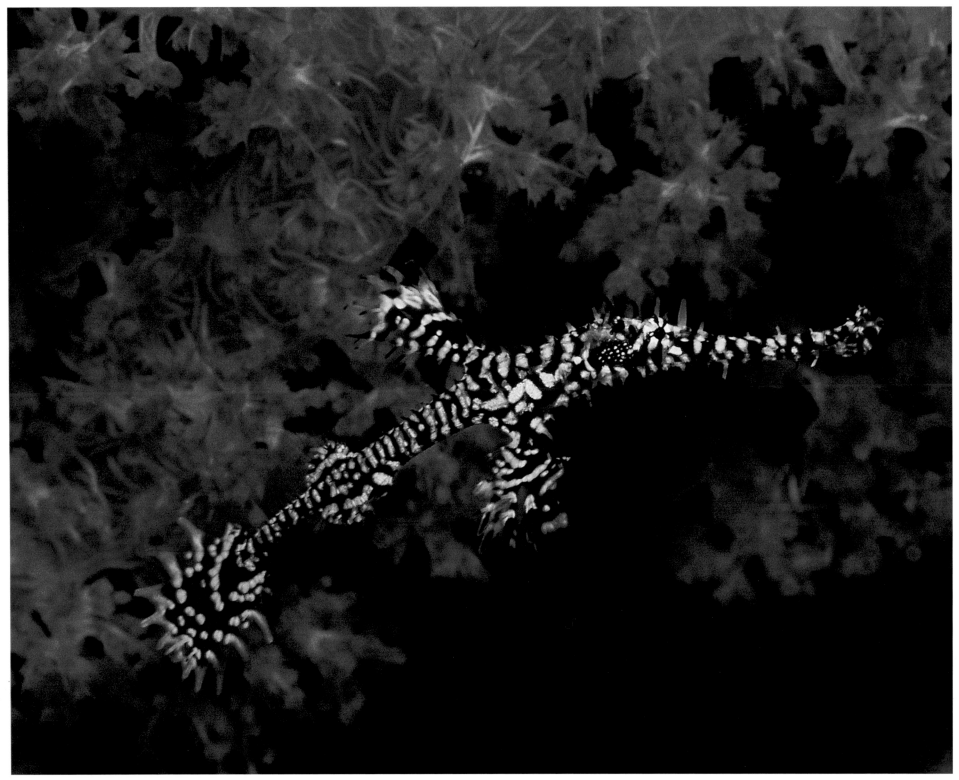

Ghost Pipefish

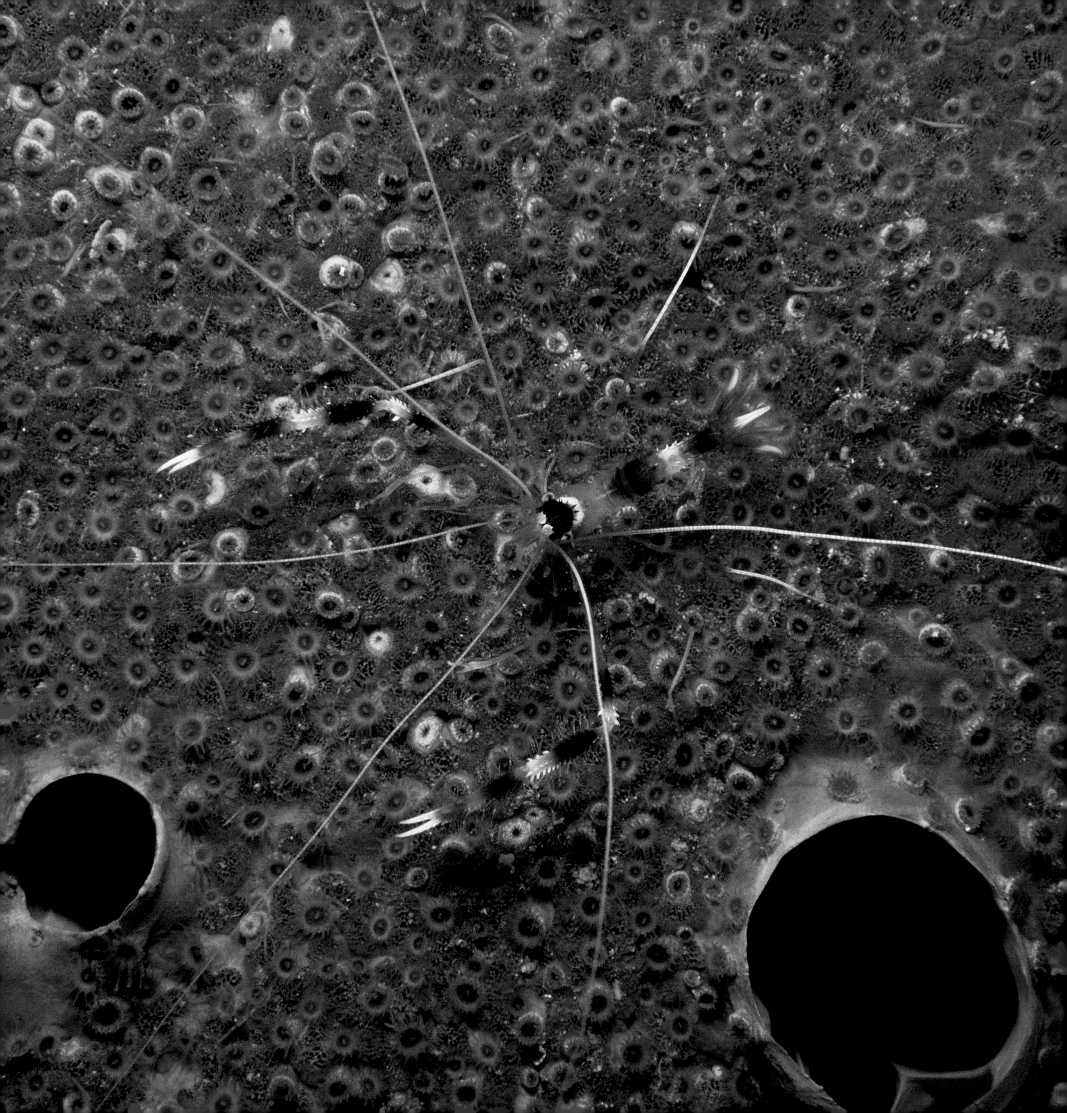

Green Spotted Nudibranch

The camera triggered my curiosity. I discovered that the smaller creatures were more interesting and more colorful than the larger animals. But the brilliant colors of the little reef inhabitants are masked to the human eye by the water's effect on the rainbow spectrum. Not until these colors are kindled by strobes and brought to life in the photofinishing process does one realize what nature has gifted these creatures.

I abandoned the buddy system as it was far too confining for my narrow focus, and I slowed way down to enjoy the solitary serenity of the reef.

Sharpnose Puffer

Arrow Crabs (above and right)

As my subject matter grew smaller and smaller, my equipment needed to become more sophisticated. I enlisted the expertise of Chris Newbert, whose own books of underwater photography, "Within a Rainbowed Sea" and "In a Sea of Dreams," are the gold standard.

Newbert recommended the Nikon F4 and a Nexus underwater housing. I chose a strobe system manufactured by Ikelite, coincidentally in my hometown – Indianapolis, Indiana. My lens of choice is a 105-millimeter macro supplemented with a teleconverter and diopters for greater magnification.

Sea Whip Gobies on Soft Coral

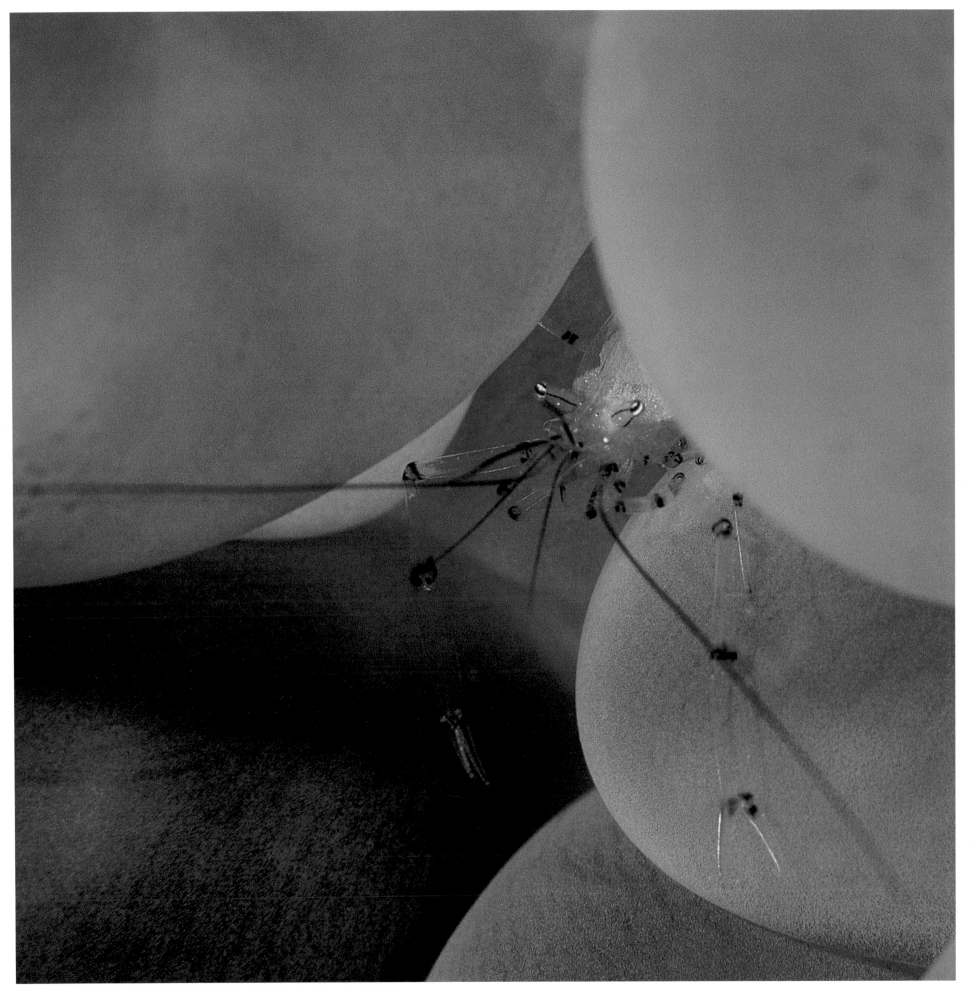

Shrimp on Bubble Coral

Anemone Shrimp (above and right)

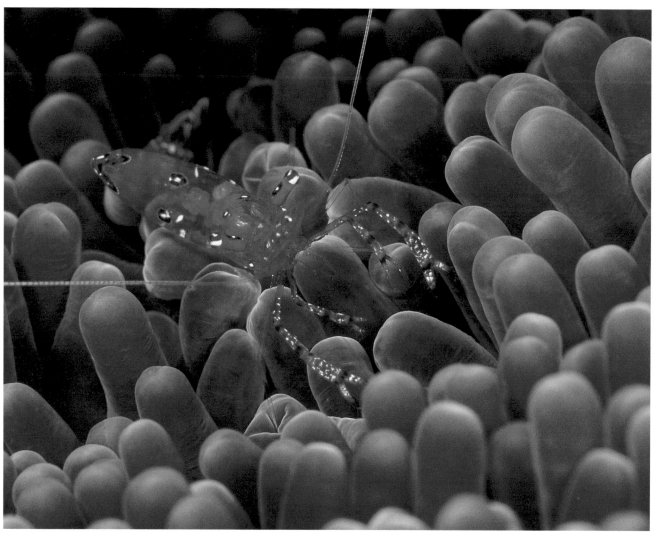

Cleaner Shrimp on Disc Anemone

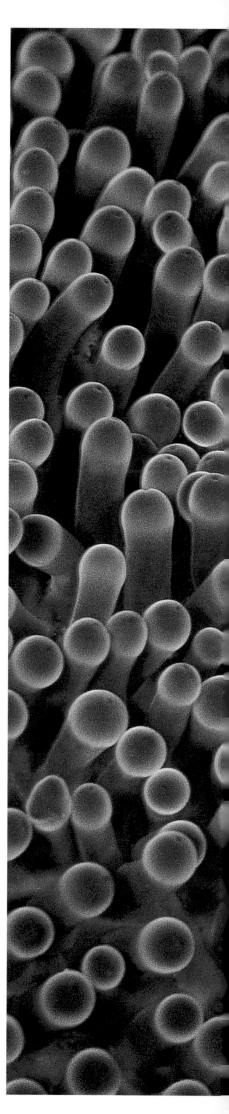

Anemone Shrimp

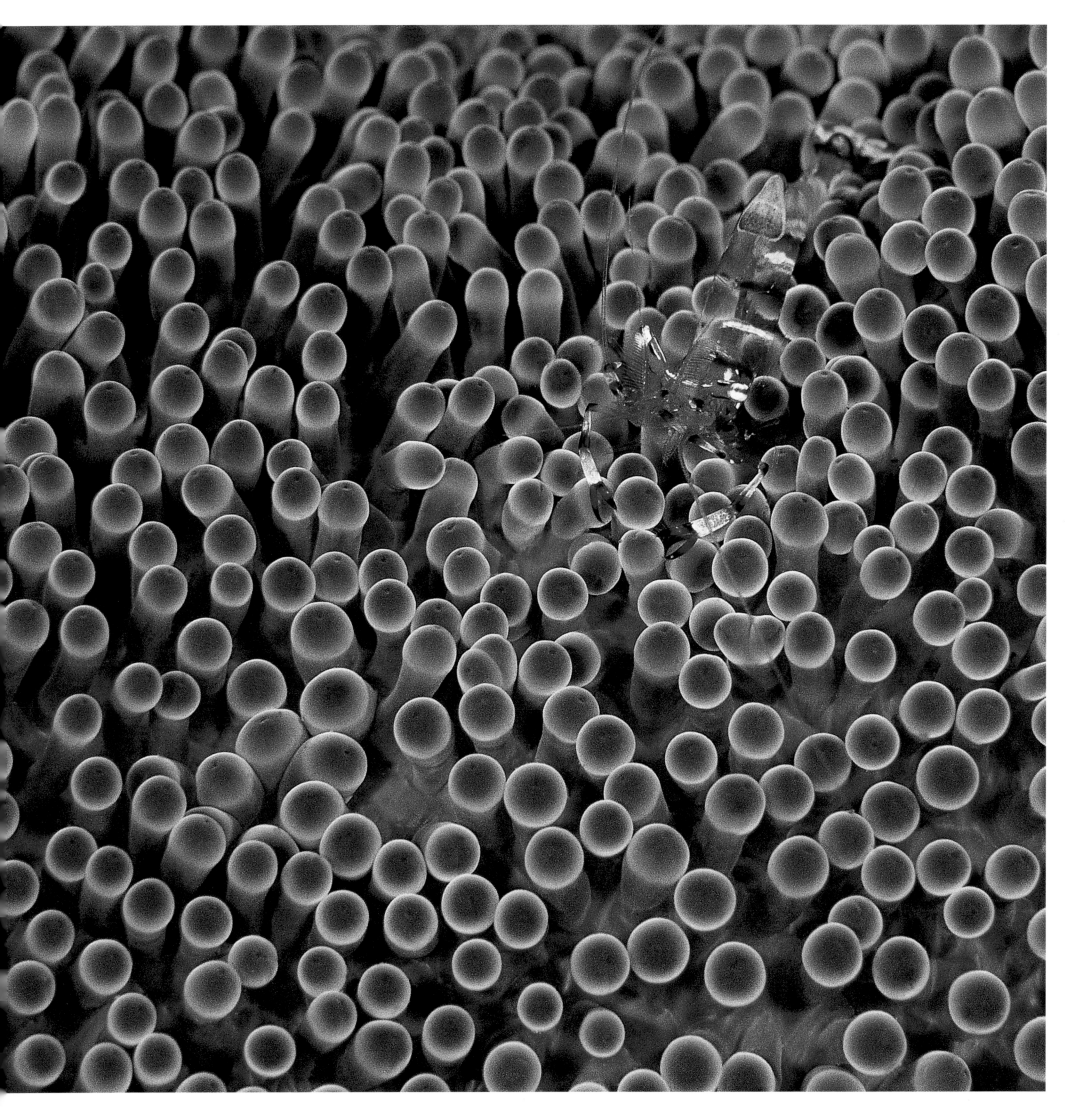

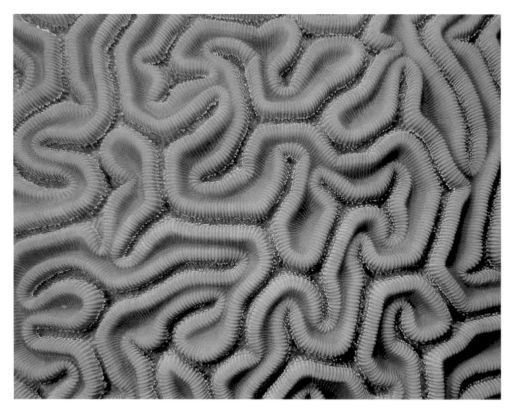

Brain coral is abundant along the reef and few divers hesitate long enough to examine it.

Too bad. Look deep within the recesses of brain coral and a triplefin blenny might stare right back at you.

Brain Coral

Triplefin Blenny in Brain Coral (above and right)

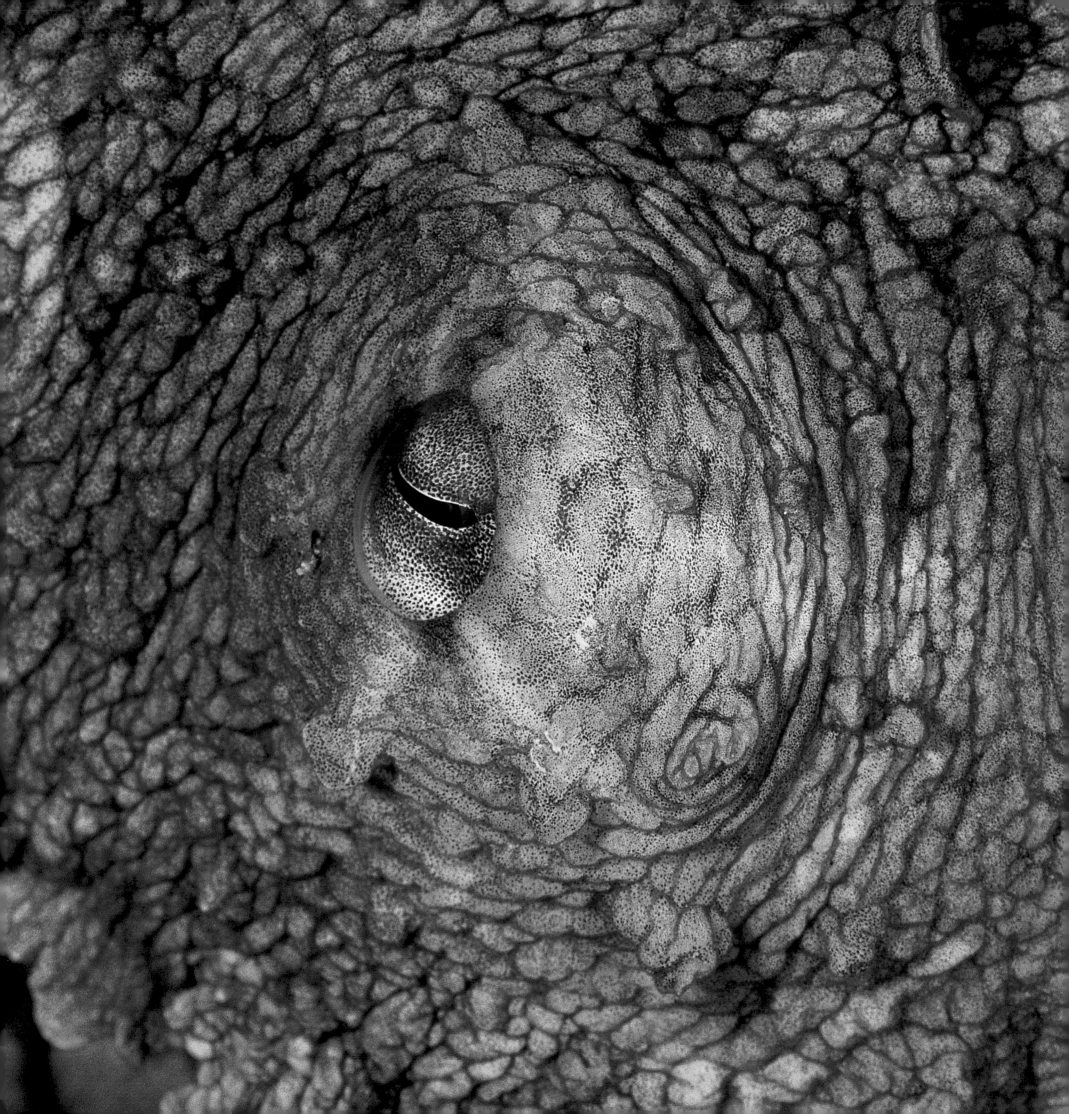

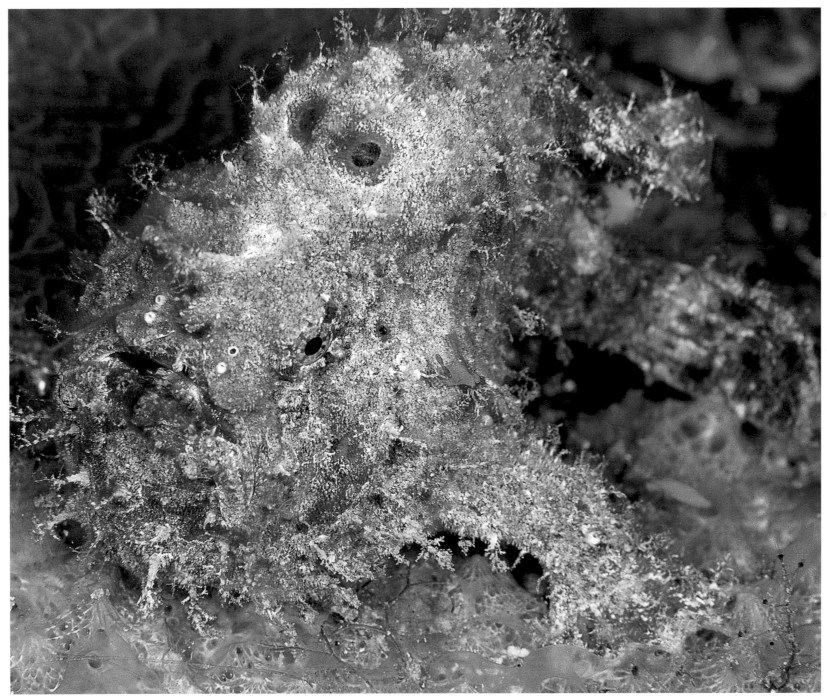

Frogfish

Many reef creatures have wonderful abilities to change form and color. I have often been fooled. On a dive in Bonaire off the coast of Venezuela, I motioned to my friend Alex Nelson to photograph a particularly interesting species. I helped him set up his camera and strobes and guided him into position to fire the shutter release. Later that day, I commented on what a beautiful frogfish we had found. Alex replied, "What frogfish?" Not until he viewed the photograph did he realize he had taken a picture of a camouflaged frogfish.

I also took one. Quick, where are its eyes? Look again.

Turn the page for a closer look.

Frogfish

Firefish

When I slipped beneath the water for the obligatory dive at the Kralendijk Town Pier in
Bonaire, I had low expectations. I was stunned by the splendor of the orange tubastria
and Christmas tree worms, open and inviting. The pier was lit by brilliant, orange flame.
It's surprising that the dive pressure on this site has not damaged the marine life;
instead, these corals impress a new group of divers every evening.

Orange Tubastria (left and above)

Christmas Tree Worms amid Orange Tubastria

Christmas Tree Worm

Squat Anemone Shrimp

File Clam

Settling down on a promising reef in Islamorada, I noticed the tentacles of a file clam barely protruding from its mantle. The file clam inhabits a nondescript mantle 2-3 inches wide that, when closed, hardly rates a second glance. Often, the file clam is attached to the reef in a narrow crevice or recess and is out of view of even the most observant diver.

File Clam (above and right)

On rare occasions, however, the file clam is accessible by camera and, when it begins to open its mantle, the photographer is rewarded with red, orange or white tentacles and equally colorful valves. The trick is to time the shutter release to the moment the file clam is open the widest, exposing its valves and tentacles. This skittish creature will shut tight the instant the strobe is fired.

When threatened, the file clam darts into a crevice by rapidly snapping its valves open and shut to expel water – literally jet-propelling itself to safety.

photo by Greg Maurer (background removed to enhance image)

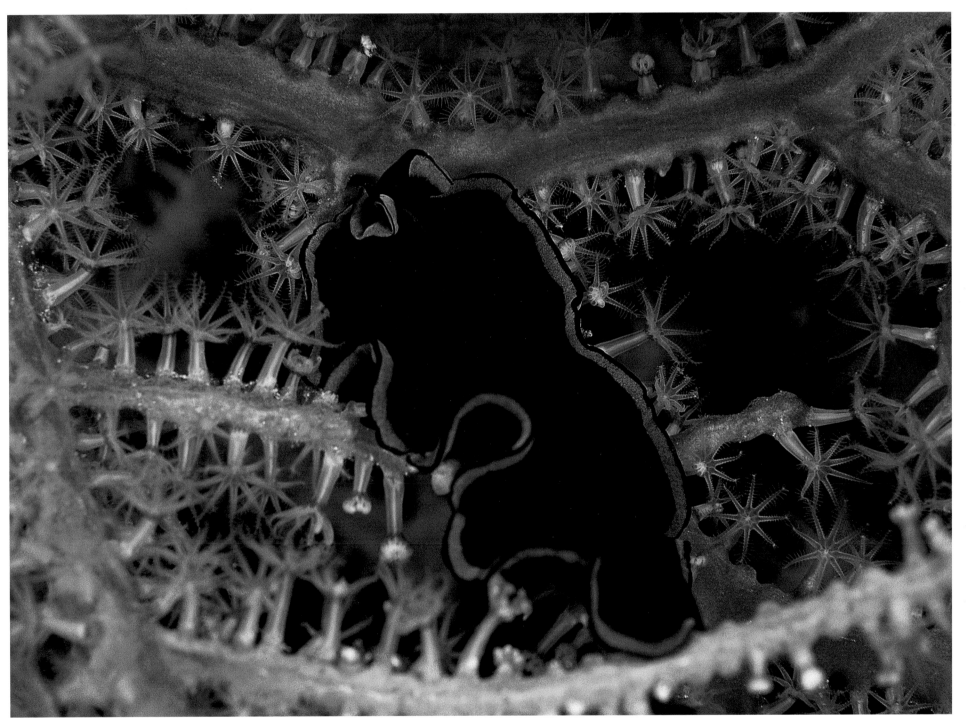

Nudibranch on Soft Coral

Goby on Soft Coral

Tridacna Clam interior

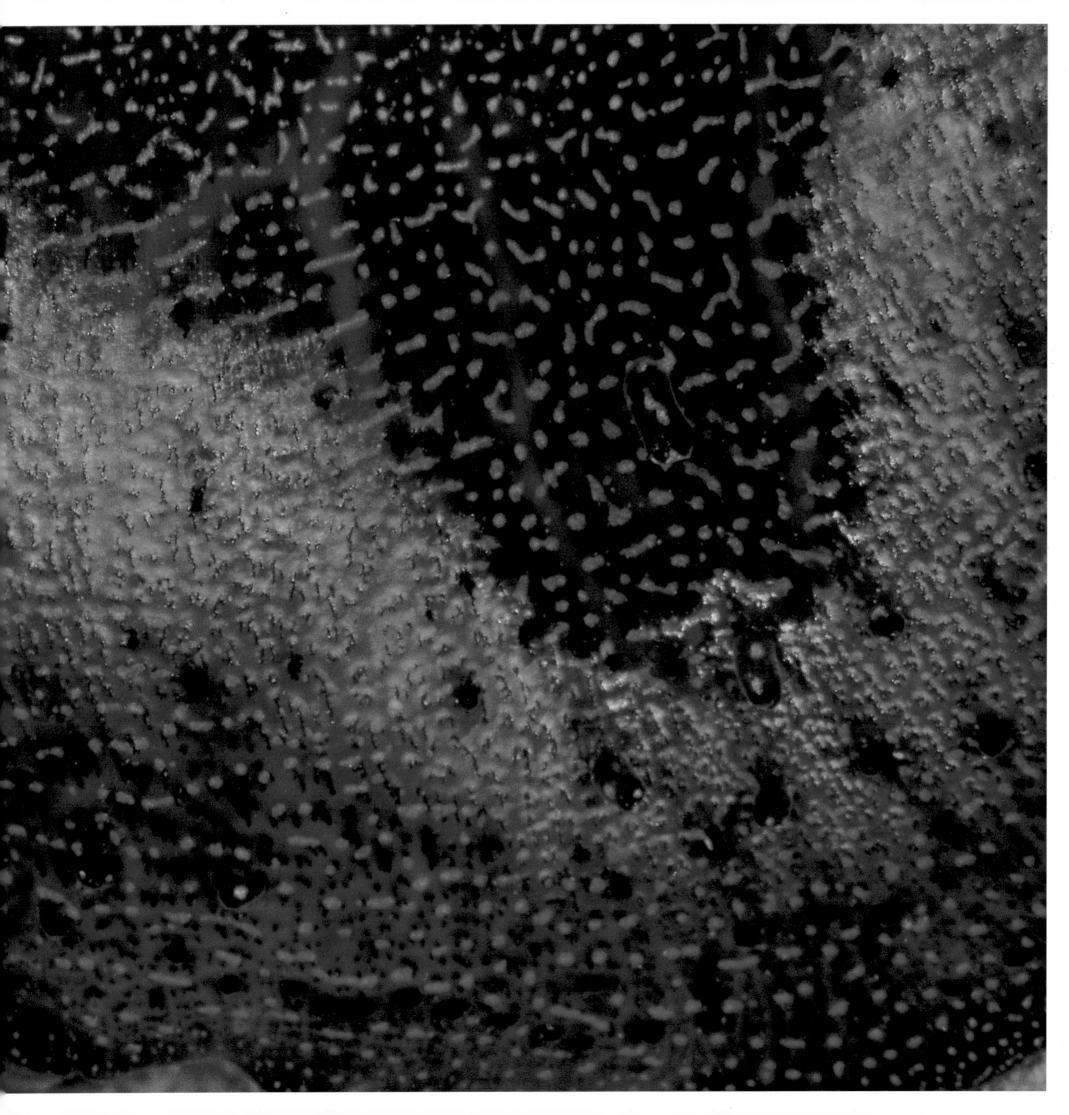

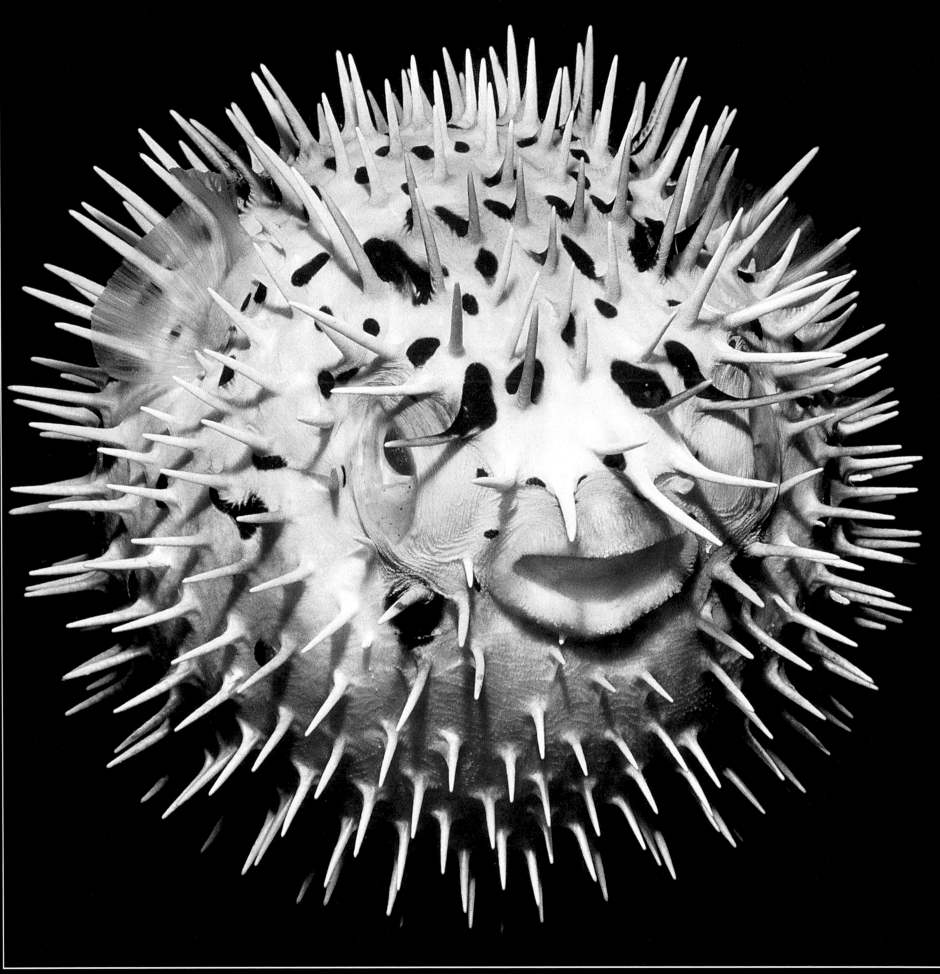

Porcupinefish (above and right)

The porcupinefish inflates to protect itself from predators. Its eyes sparkle with mystery, as you can see.

Shrimp on Wire Coral

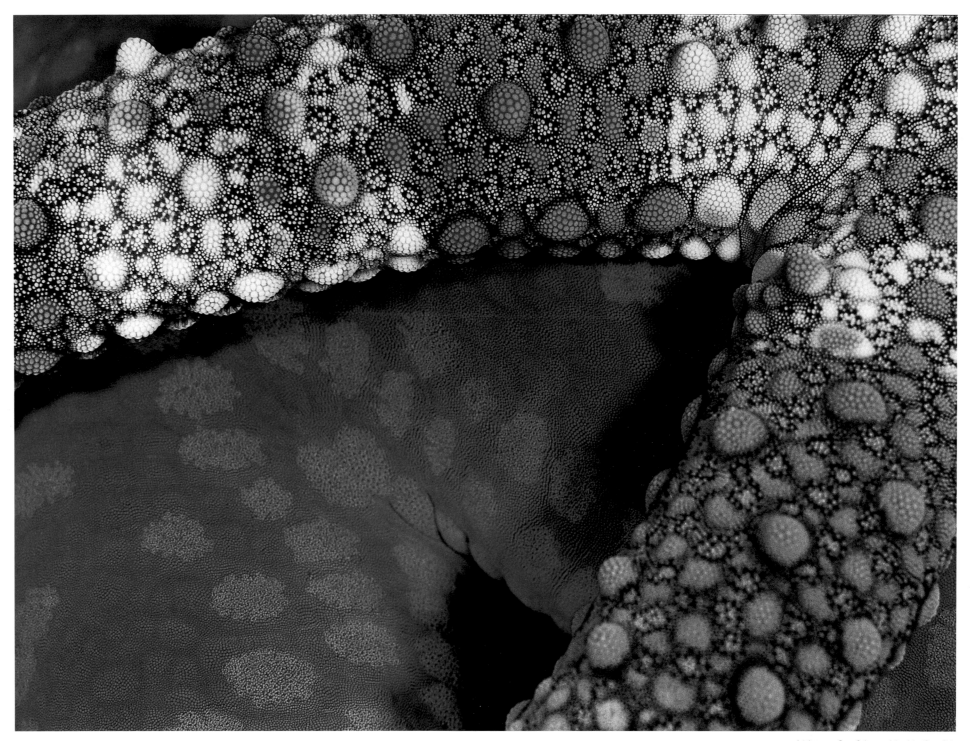

Watson Starfish on Linckia Starfish

Orange Ball Anemone

Diana's Hogfish and Soft Coral

It was nighttime in Beqa Lagoon, off the southern coast of Fiji — time for the brilliant soft corals to show off. There are more varieties and nuances of color in these corals than anywhere in the world. Every movement of my nightlight sparked another brilliant shade. Nowhere in the world are the "Water Colors" more captivating.

One photo revealed a bonus. Notice the juvenile Diana's hogfish in the image above.

Soft Coral (above and right)

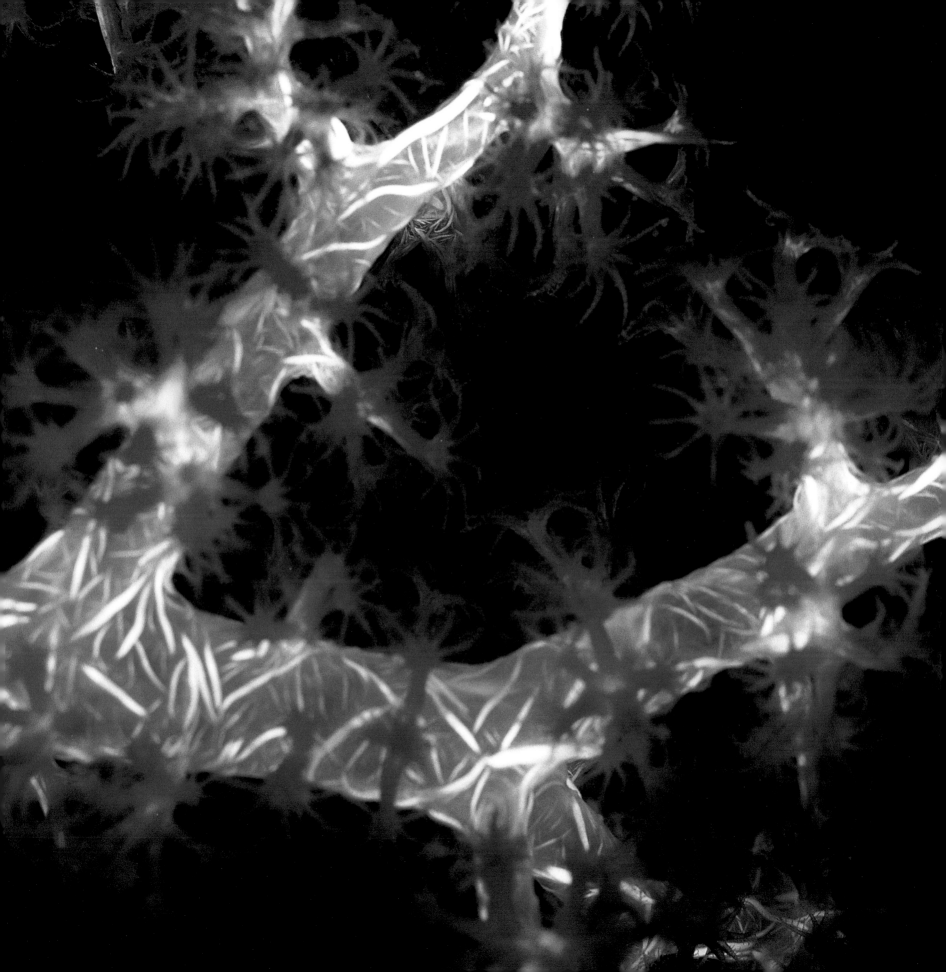

Soft Coral (above and right)

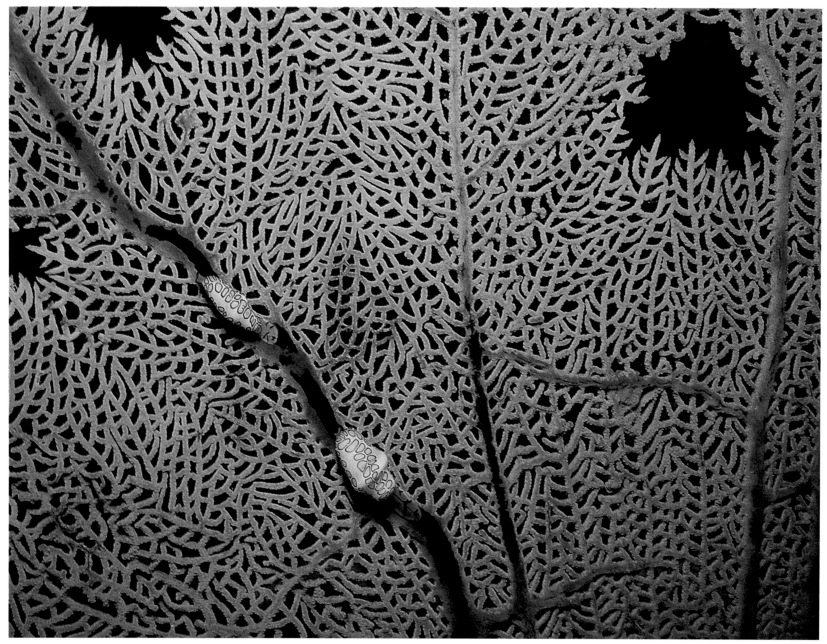

Flamingo Tongue Cowries on Sea Fan

Flamingo Tongue Cowrie

Flamingo tongue cowries are plentiful on the reef; usually, they're feeding on sea fans.

Flamingo Tongue Cowrie on Orange Sponge

Ghost Pipefish

Axelrod's Blenny

Glass Shrimp

I was curious about a National Geographic photograph taken in New Guinea by David Doubilet, whose work I've often enjoyed. It was a portrait of a mantis shrimp accompanied by a description of this dangerous and odd-looking creature's ability to inflict significant harm on prey and potential predators, including humans. The article reported that one unfortunate diver who attempted to handle this creature lost a finger to amputation. The animal has tremendous striking power that it uses to smash crabs and snails. A mantis shrimp was definitely on my list when I visited Papua New Guinea.

In about 20 feet of water, I noticed an unusual hole on the sandy bottom. Hovering nearby, I dropped in a small stick and heard a resounding crash as something struck at the intrusion. I was astounded when a mantis shrimp marched right out of its hole with stick in claw. I was so surprised I didn't have my camera ready. I watched the shrimp's miraculous eyes search for the source of the intrusion — big round eyes that appeared to be bisected by a band and that moved independently of each other. In a second, the mantis shrimp disappeared down the hole. I steadied my camera and inserted the stick again. When the shrimp emerged this time, I was ready.

Mantis Shrimp

Find an old shell. Turn it over. You may be greeted by a hermit crab. The hermit crab finds an empty shell to live in until it is ready to molt. Then, it selects a larger one to fit its growing body.

Hermit Crab (this page and right)

Nudibranch

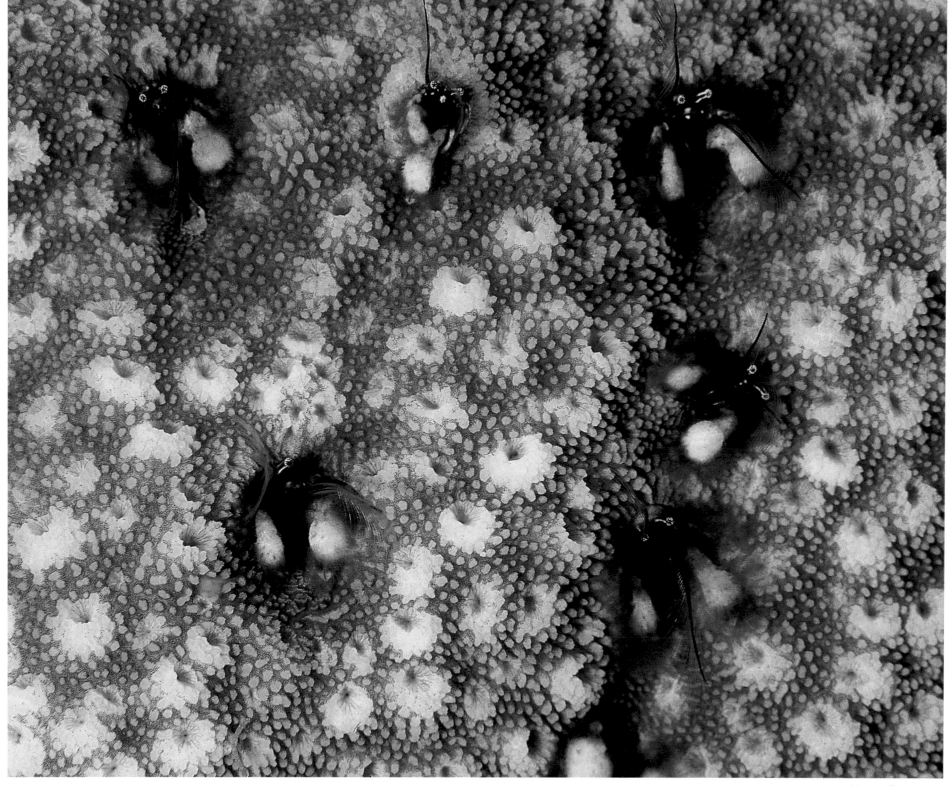

Hermit Crab colony

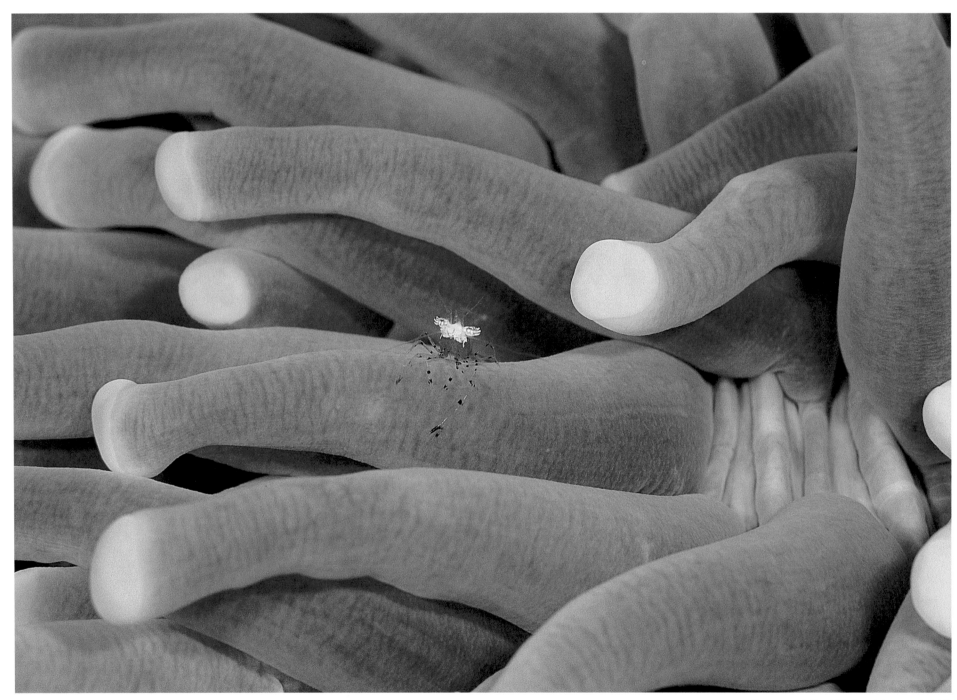

Commensal Coral Shrimp (above and right)

This blenny kept popping in and out so fast I could not get a shot. Finally, it hesitated just long enough to kiss me goodbye.

Bicolor Blenny

Spiny Blenny

I studied this sea fan for some time, detecting nothing remarkable. Suddenly, I noticed movement. As the animal swung around to face me, I lifted my camera and discovered through the magnifying lens a pygmy sea horse no larger than a grain of rice.

Pygmy Sea Horse

Peekaboo.

Peppermint Shrimp in Vase Sponge

Pixy Hawkfish

Hinge-beak Shrimp

Gorgonian

Longnose Hawkfish on Gorgonian

Blenny

The sweet lips is in constant motion. It could be nicknamed "The Mad Hatter".
It really tests a photographer's patience. After an interminable chase, this sweet lips
finally paused for less than a second. One click and it was off again.

Sweet Lips

algae-covered Reef Crab

Hermit Crab

Yellowhead Jawfish (above and right)

While gliding slowly along open terrain between reefs, I noticed a face peeking at me. Just a face. I stopped and waited.

It was a yellowhead jawfish, who danced for me a few seconds before returning to a safer haven.

Hermit Crab

Maroon Clownfish

The tentacles of the anemone are dangerous to most small fish, but the clownfish lives within the anemone and acquires an immunity to its sting. In return for protection, some species of clownfish feed the anemone.

As in all good marriages, both parties are aglow.

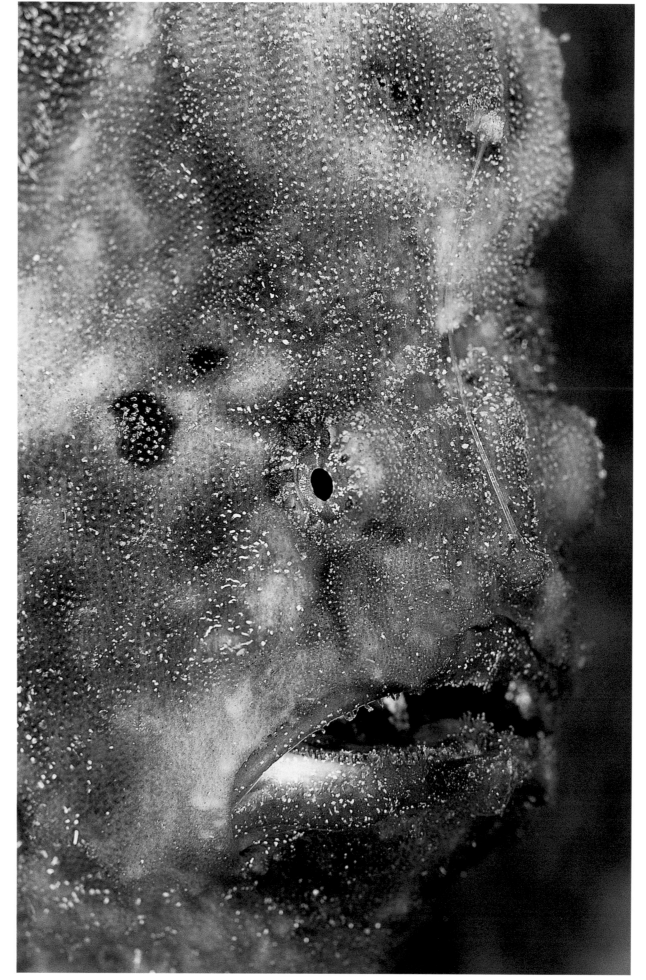

Frogfish

Soft Coral

Frogfish

Bearded Fireworm

Look but don't touch is the best advice on the reef. It is especially so with the bearded fireworm, which can deliver a powerful sting.

Feather Duster Worms

Hinge-beak Shrimp

Twin Spot Gobies

Flowerpot Coral

The spotted moray eel has cruised into the local cleaning
station. How many shrimp can you count?

Spotted Moray Eel and friends

Moray Eels

Anemone Shrimp

Scorpion Fish

A Patriotic Experience

Songs like "This Is My Country" and "God Bless America" are especially moving to me. I've always enjoyed this genre of music, especially for its melodies. Until a fateful day in 1990, though, these songs did not evoke emotions of enthusiastic patriotism – the goose-pimple effect.

The date is not difficult to remember. It was September 4, Janie's birthday. We were scuba diving with some friends in Eleuthera, one of the beautiful Bahama islands, and looking forward to that special combination of blue water, triple-digit visibility and exciting marine life.

Cleaner Minic

Basket Starfish

Pink-tipped Anemone

Triplefin Blenny

Merlet Scorpion Fish

Skunk Clownfish in Anemone

We planned a deep first dive with appropriate safety stops for decompression during our ascent. The dive was routine until I elected to abort much of the decompression stage due to the presence of a hungry shark agitated by a bloodied fish on the end of a fisherman's spear.

Back aboard our boat, we were in the midst of laughing about the ones who got away (this time we were talking about ourselves) when I suddenly collapsed from paralysis of my right leg. I had spinal-cord-related decompression sickness, an often life-threatening form of what is commonly called "the bends."

Chemistry and physics majors know the bends is a direct and dire consequence of Henry's law. In simple terms, the bends occurs when nitrogen forms bubbles in tissues and blood vessels. The bubbles expand upon ascent much like when a bottle of soda is opened.

Scorpion Fish

Striped Coral Goby in Bubble Coral

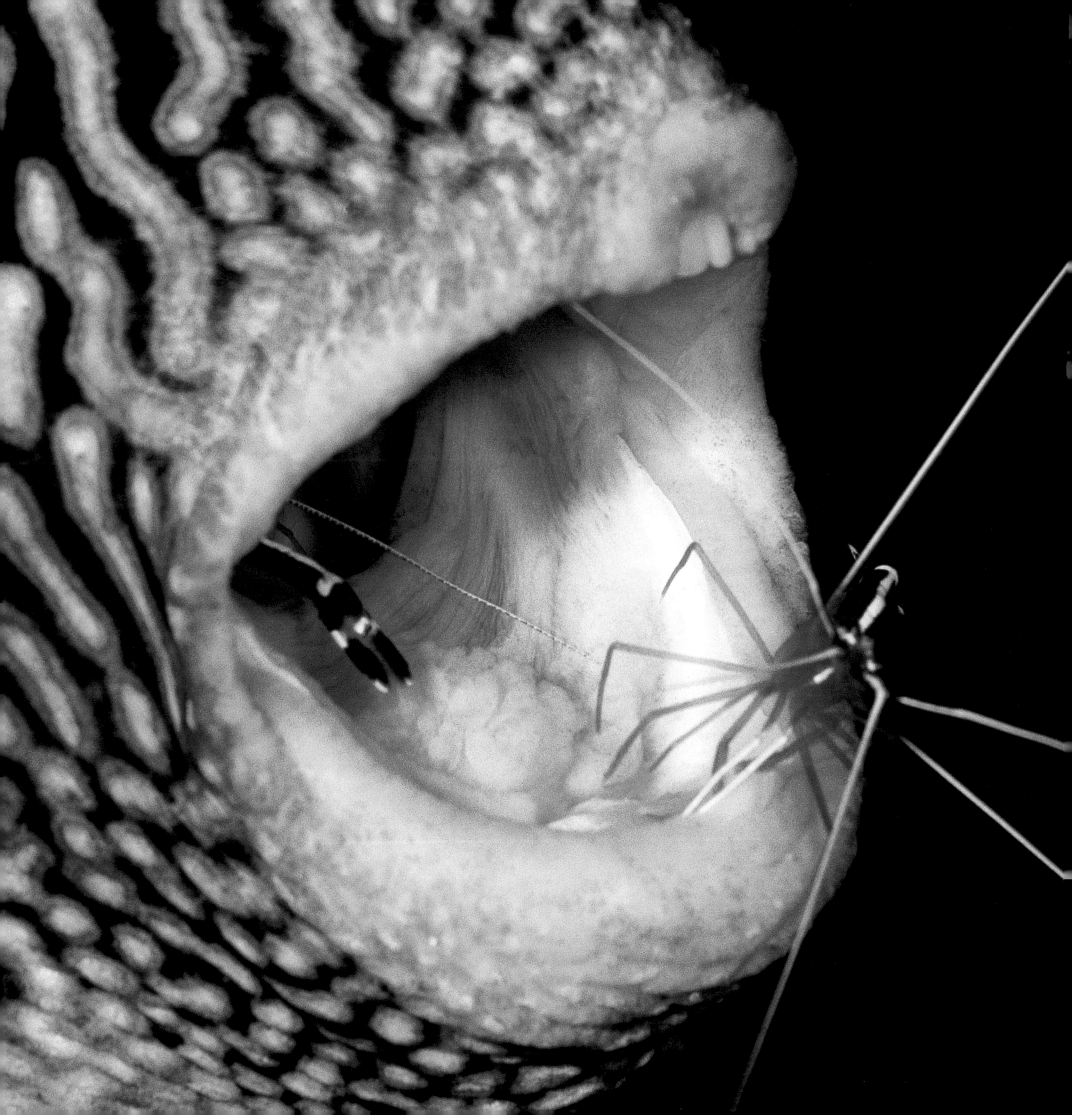

After about an hour, my leg was able to function. But because symptoms of decompression sickness tend to reappear, I needed to be evacuated to a recompression chamber without delay. I was advised over the telephone by doctors at the University of Miami to take oxygen and drink a lot of water. While breathing oxygen and drinking water by the gallon forced down my throat by my wife, I waited for a plane that was dispatched by the U.S. Coast Guard to evacuate me to the recompression chamber in Miami.

As soon as the jet arrived, I boarded and was immediately wired with various monitors and contraptions by virtue of which I was completely immobile. The jet flew at low altitude and was pressurized to sea level so as not to exacerbate my problem.

Crocodile Fish

Ribbon Eel

Mushroom Anemone

Halfway into the trip, the gallons of water I had ingested took effect. I was in excruciating pain from a tremendous urge to go to the bathroom. Think of your worst experience in this regard, whether it was in 4th grade spelling class or a rush-hour traffic jam, and multiply that pressure times 10. You will understand how I felt.

When the plane finally arrived at a military base in Miami and all my wires were unhooked, I dashed across the tarmac and into the first rest room I could find. The medical technicians were in hot pursuit.

With that job taken care of, I surrendered and was taken by ambulance to the University of Miami hospital emergency room. The first words out of the mouth of the physician who met us at the door were, "I'm going to need a urine specimen."

Trumpet Fish

Damselfish

A combination of bad luck and bad judgment put my life in jeopardy, but the USA was there for me. Few nations in the world would take such care about a single citizen so as to send a rescue squad to a foreign country.

Indeed, patriotic songs now give me the goose-pimple effect. This *is* my country. God bless America.

photo by Janie Maurer

ACKNOWLEDGMENTS:

Underwater photography is by nature a solitary endeavor. Perhaps that is one of the reasons I enjoy it so much. The making of this book, however, was a team effort.

I am extremely grateful for the hard work of this team, particularly the design and production experts at the *Indianapolis Business Journal* — Jo Payton, creative director, and Pat Keiffner, director of production/contract publishing. Jo reviewed hundreds of photographs and assisted me in the difficult task of eliminating the ones that did not make the book. She then artfully arranged these pages to provide a smooth flow. Jo was also responsible for the artwork on the jacket and throughout the book. Pat was the captain of the team and carefully guided this volume through the layout, scanning and printing processes. Completing the production team was Ann Finch, copy editor of the *Indianapolis Business Journal*, who provided many hours of assistance in converting my dictation into readable text. Her numerous ideas were invaluable.

Thank you to experts Stuart Keefer, senior aquarist of The Indianapolis Zoological Society, and Dawn Franke, aquarist, and Ernie Sawyer, senior aquarist, of Shedd Aquarium for assistance in creature identification.

A special thanks to Jeffrey P. Bonner, president and CEO of the St. Louis Zoo, and Michael Crowther, president and CEO of The Indianapolis Zoological Society, for their encouragement.

My skill was polished at the feet of some of our nation's best photo professionals — Chris McLaughlin, Marcio Handler and Chris Newbert. All have been gracious with suggestions and constructive criticism.

Many thanks to the underwater equipment professionals at Ikelite, especially Ike Brigham, who has always been available to solve equipment woes for me.

Graphic Arts Center Indianapolis has brought my photographs to life through the scanning and printing processes. I appreciate the company's patience and careful attention to detail.

I am indebted to Firehouse Image Center, Indianapolis' premier professional lab, and Sally Corman for photofinishing needs and particularly for enthusiastic cooperation in the various charitable endeavors relating to my photographs over the years.

A note of appreciation for Brett Waller, immediate past director of the Indianapolis Museum of Art, and his wife, Mary Lou, a noted artist, for their discerning eye and design sensibility in the layout of this book.

I gratefully acknowledge the cheerful support of my two executive assistants, Sharon Miller and Marla Smith. Marla's admiration for my work has given me courage to present this to the public.

A special thank you to Bob Mayes, my first scuba-diving instructor.

This book is dedicated to my beautiful wife, Janie. I wanted you to see what she looks like but she is a bit shy. Can you find her?